EARTH AFIRE!
Volcanoes and Their Activity

By the Same Author

What to Eat and Why, *The Science of Nutrition*
Earth in Motion, *The Concept of Plate Tectonics*
Nickels, Dimes, and Dollars, *How Currency Works*

R.V. Fodor

EARTH AFIRE!

Volcanoes and Their Activity

illustrated with photographs and diagrams

William Morrow and Company
New York 1981

The author is grateful to Professor M.F. Sheridan, volcanologist, Arizona State University, for his review of the text.

Library of Congress Cataloging in Publication Data

Fodor, R. V.
    Earth afire!
    Includes index.
    Summary: Discusses the formation of volcanoes, some famous ones, types of eruptions, and the possible benefits of these spectacular phenomena of nature.
    1. Volcanoes—Juvenile literature. [1.Volcanoes] I. Title.
QE521.3.F63   551.2′1   81–3984
ISBN 0–688–00706–6   AACR2
ISBN 0–688–00707–4 (lib. bdg.)

Illustration Credits

Bureau of Mineral Resources, Canberra City, Australia, 39, 41, 50; J.C. Coleman, Battelle Memorial Institute, Pacific Northwest Laboratories, Richland, Washington, 73; R.V. Fodor, 23 (bottom), 26, 42; J.C. Holden, 20, 22, 24, 48, 57, 58, 59, 61, 62, 63, 66, 67, 68, 74, 84, 87; National Aeronautics and Space Administration, 29; National Oceanic and Atmospheric Administration: National Earth and Satellite Service, 75; Oregon State Department of Transportation, 27; Oregon State Highway Department, 47; Pacific Gas and Electric, 82; M.F. Sheridan, 16; Sigurdur Thorarinsson, 64; Underwood and Underwood, Library of Congress, 38; U.S. Air Force, 15, 36, 54; U.S. Geological Survey, 10, 12, 21, 23 (top), 31, 34, 44, 55, 71, 76, 77, 80, 88; Weyerhaeuser, Tacoma, Washington, 13

Contents

◀ I ▶

Restless Mountains

The volcano Mount Saint Helens awoke from a 123-year sleep on March 20, 1980, with a small earthquake that rattled its lofty peak. That quake gave the first clue to the dangerously high pressures inside. It also set the stage for an explosion that was powerful enough to blow off the mountaintop two months later.

More earthquakes quickly followed the first one and Earth scientists moved in to place sensitive instruments around the mountain. Although Mount Saint Helens had not erupted since 1857, the scientists knew that it might be preparing to explode again. They wanted to keep close watch on its behavior by measuring the rumblings inside.

In only a few days, their instruments showed that the quakes were growing stronger. Some were large enough to trigger snow avalanches off the mountain slopes. And at times the earthquakes were so severe

A steam eruption from the summit of Mount Saint Helens
in April, 1980.

that the scientific instruments became unreadable. But
there was no volcanic eruption.

Then, on March 27, one week after its awakening,
Mount Saint Helens produced its first explosive sights

and sounds. Out of the volcano, a cloud of hot steam and ash burst skyward and sculptured a deep bowl-shaped hole, or crater, in the mountaintop, eighty meters across and fifty meters deep.

By the next day, Mount Saint Helens had exploded several dozen more times, and the column of steam and ash rose three kilometers above the volcano. Eruptions continued over the following days, and a second crater grew at the top. Flickering blue flames of burning volcanic gases jumped from one crater to the other. The heat melted the snow and ice covering the mountaintop, and meltwater sent thick, damaging mudflows sliding down the volcano's flanks.

Concerned for their safety, local residents began leaving. At the same time, however, curious tourists were gathering to watch the violent, yet spectacular natural display.

The volcanic activity continued for several weeks, much to the delight of tourists, newsmen, and photographers. The bursting clouds of ash, steam, and other gases and the earthquakes offered them exciting entertainment. To obtain better views, some people flew over the volcano in planes and helicopters. Others actually hiked up the mountainside for a breathtaking look inside. Still others used the attraction to make money selling tourist items, such as T-shirts with "I survived Mount St. Helens" printed across the front.

Mount Saint Helens blows its top on May 18, 1980.

At the end of April, the volcano became drastically more dangerous as Mount Saint Helens presented new displays of the explosive pressures inside. The number and strength of the earthquakes had increased, and the north slope of the volcano began to bulge like a giant balloon, expanding about two meters per day. Scientists said that the bulge occurred because magma, or molten rock, was moving up into the volcano in preparation for a violent escape.

Three weeks later, on the morning of May 18, Mount Saint Helens rocked Washington State. People 300 kilometers away heard the blast. Its power scattered the mountaintop across the countryside, leaving the volcano 425 meters smaller than it was. That force, scientists estimate, equaled the power of the largest hydrogen bomb ever exploded.

The energy of the eruption stripped nearby trees bare and snapped them like toothpicks. People and wildlife

The force of the May 18 eruption felled trees as though they were toothpicks.

in the area were killed instantly either by the force of the blast or by the heat, which reached over 500 degrees Celsius. Survivors also reported that poisonous gases made breathing difficult. And hot ash and rock rained down over the surrounding area from a thick, black cloud. The falling debris buried the land under a layer several centimeters thick. In some areas, rock and ash from the landslides and the eruption filled rivers and streams, causing waterways to plow through valleys like walls of wet cement.

Over the volcano, the plume of ash and steam rose fifteen kilometers high, growing like a giant cauliflower. Winds carried the smallest particles and spread them far across Washington and into neighboring Oregon. Ashfall at Yakima, Washington, for example—one hundred and fifty kilometers away—reached ten to thirteen centimeters deep.

Near the volcano, dozens of people remain missing and are presumed buried beneath the ash and mudflows. One of them is geologist David Johnston, who was working at an observation point eight kilometers away from the volcano on May 18. His last words into his radio transmitter—"Vancouver, Vancouver. This is it!"—indicate that he saw the explosion happening.

The disaster at Mount Saint Helens took the country by surprise. Not only did it claim human lives, it also ruined hundreds of millions of dollars' worth of

Static electricity builds over erupting Vesuvius in 1944.

timber, timberland, crops, and personal property. Clean-up costs, too, amounted to millions of dollars. These monumental losses, however, are only a small part of the destruction that the world's active volcanoes have caused humankind since its beginning. For example, one estimate numbers the lives lost to volcanic eruptions over the past 500 years at 200,000.

The size of the tragedies caused by some volcanic eruptions has established them as historic events. The best known probably is the eruption of Vesuvius, in

A victim of the A.D. 79 eruption of Vesuvius on Pompeii.

Italy, in A.D. 79. That blast probably equaled the Mount Saint Helens explosion in strength, and it remains infamous for burying the Roman city of Pompeii and many of its 20,000 residents. And in 1883, Krakatoa—located between Java and Sumatra—exploded so violently that people 5,000 kilometers away heard it. The eruption sent tsunamis (tidal waves) across the Indian Ocean, drowning 36,000 people in 295 neighboring Indonesian villages. Over two thirds of the island that Krakatoa occupied disappeared in that blast.

About 500 volcanoes across the Earth are active,

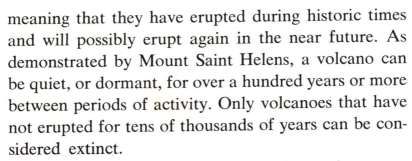

meaning that they have erupted during historic times and will possibly erupt again in the near future. As demonstrated by Mount Saint Helens, a volcano can be quiet, or dormant, for over a hundred years or more between periods of activity. Only volcanoes that have not erupted for tens of thousands of years can be considered extinct.

But not all active volcanoes are destructive to society. Some erupt under the sea as Capelinhos volcano, near the Azores in the Atlantic Ocean, did in 1957. Others, such as those of the Aleutian Islands, Alaskan peninsula, and in parts of Alaska, erupt harmlessly on islands or in areas far from settlements.

Active volcanoes in the Mediterranean Sea surrounded the centers of the early Roman and Greek cultures. Besides Vesuvius, there was Mount Etna, Stromboli, Santorini, and the volcano that lends its name to all others in the world—Vulcano. The Romans living near Vulcano believed that its eruptions came from the vent of a chimney leading down to the forge of Vulcan, the blacksmith of the Roman gods. Vulcan supposedly made the armor of the gods and the thunderbolts of Jupiter.

The proximity of the early Greeks and Romans to active volcanoes led them to make the first scientific speculations about volcanoes: what caused them to erupt and what the eruptions indicated about the Earth.

The earliest explanations for volcanism, however, were fantasy compared to what we know about volcanoes today. Plato (427-347 B.C.), for example, believed that volcanoes were somehow tied to channelways below the Earth's surface in which streams of air, fire, and water moved about. And Aristotle (385-322 B.C.) thought eruptions were fiery "pent-up" winds in the Earth that occasionally escaped to cause earthquakes and volcanism.

Credit for the first authentic contribution to the science of volcanology goes to the Roman author Pliny the Younger. He described in writing how the A.D. 79 eruption of Vesuvius smothered the land with "black pieces of burning rock" falling from a dark cloud that turned daytime into night and claimed the life of his uncle, Pliny the Elder.

Hundreds of years later, however, during the 1700's and 1800's, accurate knowledge about volcanoes began growing. And by the early 1900's, volcanologists greatly advanced their science by setting up observatories near some highly active volcanoes. The Italians established the Vesuvian Observatory, and the Japanese watched over their Mount Asama. Russian scientists began studies of the volcanoes on their Kamchatka peninsula, and American volcanologists organized the Hawaiian Volcano Observatory, which today still overlooks Kilauea volcano.

Through observatories around the world, scientists acquired firsthand, detailed knowledge on every aspect of volcanic eruptions. They determined that the temperatures of the molten rock that pours from volcanoes can be 1,100 degrees Celsius and that the gases spewed out during eruptions include water vapor, chlorine, sulfur, and carbon dioxide.

The observations also led to the modern understanding of the nature of a volcano. It is now known to be a cone-shaped hill or mountain built around a vent that connects with a reservoir of molten rock (magma) below the Earth's surface. The depth to the reservoir, or magma chamber, can be several kilometers.

Magma erupts from its reservoir because gases within the reservoir force it upward. It rises through zones of weakness in the overlying rock that, in effect, form a vent for escape. Upon reaching the surface, the magma either pours from the vent as a liquid or explodes into the air, where it cools and hardens as fragments. The liquid is called "lava," whereas fragments from explosively ejected magma are called "pyroclastic material."

Lava that flows across the surface eventually cools into layers of rock that increase the size of the volcano. While flowing and cooling, lava surfaces acquire different forms. One common type, known as pahoehoe (pah'-ho-e-ho-e), is a rippled or ropy surface. An-

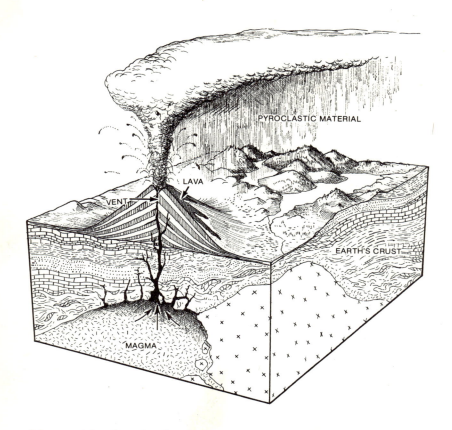

Magma rising from its chamber to erupt as lava
and pyroclastic material.

other form, known as aa (ah-ah), is jagged, and a
third form is simply blocky. Lava flowing into the sea
or erupting underwater is sometimes called "pillow"
lava because of the pillowy, lobelike forms that develop.

Pyroclastic material, too, adds to a volcano's size by
falling around the vent as individual fragments called

"bombs," "blocks," and "lapilli." Bombs and blocks are greater than sixty-four millimeters in size, and lapilli are as small as two millimeters.

Bombs are globs of magma that have acquired twisted or spherical shapes during flight or flat pie shapes upon splatting against the ground. Blocks, on the other hand, are erupted fragments of solid rock that was already part of the volcano and are, therefore, angular in shape. Lapilli can be either newly erupted magma or pre-existing solid rock. Geologists sometimes use the more casual term *cinder* for an irregularly shaped pyroclastic fragment of lapilli size.

Lava from Kilauea volcano, Hawaii,
cascades eighty meters over cliffs.

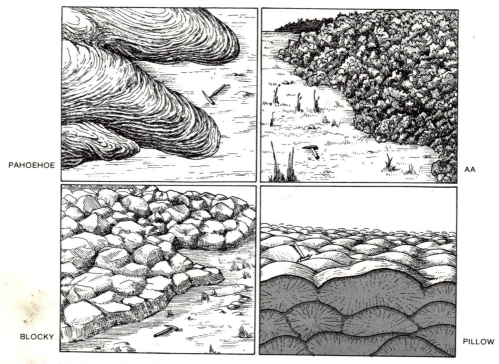

Moving and cooling lava flows acquire various surface features: pahoehoe (ropy), aa (jagged), blocky, and pillow.

The smallest pyroclastic material erupted is ash, which readily blows away with the wind before falling to the ground many kilometers away. Some pyroclastic particles are so small that winds carry them to the upper atmosphere (stratosphere), where they may circulate around the Earth for several years, as happened after the explosion of Krakatoa. So much ash blasted into the atmosphere that sunsets all over the world were

A pyroclastic eruption of bombs at Paricutín volcano
in Mexico in 1943.

A large almond-shaped bomb (center), two spheroidal bombs,
two bomb fragments, and a volcanic block (right).

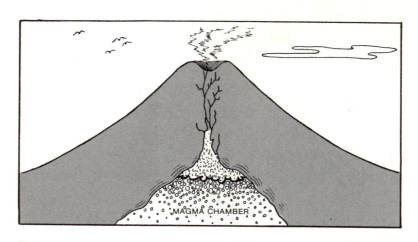

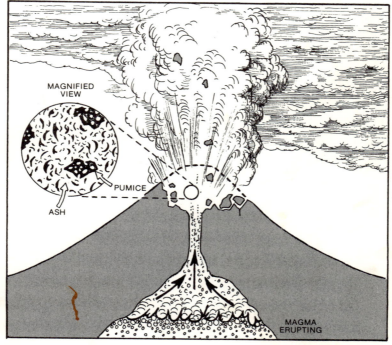

Erupting magma froth is broken into ash and pumice.

redder than usual for the following two years while the volcanic dust gradually settled to the ground.

Some pyroclastic rock resembles a sponge as it has many holes and is light enough to float on water. This rock is pumice, which is cooled magma froth, or foam, that was fragmented by volcanic eruption. A magma froth can be compared to the foam that forms when a bottle of soda is shaken. Shaking the bottle separates the gas from the liquid and produces froth at the top.

In the case of magma near the surface, gases may accumulate in the upper portion. When the magma froth erupts, most of it blows apart into small pieces, which are ash. But some remains as frothy clots that cool and become lapilli-sized particles rich with holes. The holes are bubbles of the magma froth from which the gases escaped. The walls of the bubbles are the substance that remains and forms the pumice.

Pumice was the material that buried Pompeii in A.D. 79. And, in Central America, pumice ejected from the many volcanoes has blanketed that area with layers hundreds of meters thick. Some underwater eruptions also produce pumice. In 1878, for example, an eruption in the South Pacific Ocean near the Solomon Islands cluttered the sea with so much floating pumice that ships needed several more days than normal to force their way through it.

Thick accumulations of hot ash and pumice frag-

Close-up of pumice, showing its spongelike appearance.
The thumbtack serves as a scale.

ments may eventually consolidate and become a layer of rock. This rock, however, is unlike the dense rock formed after moving lava cools. Instead, it retains a powdery, friable character. This pyroclastic rock is called "tuff."

Volcanoes have added vast amounts of rock to the

Cliffs of tuff, pumice, and ash near Crater Lake, Oregon.

26

crust of the Earth during its history. By far the greatest quantities of volcanic rock are the ocean floors, nearly all of which have come from underwater volcanoes. Ocean floor volcanic rock is many hundreds of meters thick.

Geologic investigations, the scientific studies of the Earth, have shown that volcanic rock on the continents varies widely in age. The western United States, for example, has volcanic rock that ranges from a few hundred to fifty million years in age. In North Carolina, on the other hand, volcanic rocks are about four hundred million years old. And, in Michigan, there is volcanic rock over one billion years old. Clearly, volcanoes have played big roles in the Earth's development since it formed over four billion years ago.

In recent years, United States space exploration has shown that there are volcanoes throughout the solar system. For example, volcanic rocks make up much of the moon's surface. And Mars has Olympus Mons, the largest volcano known to exist anywhere. It is twenty kilometers high and large enough to cover the State of New York. One of the most exciting space developments of the 1970's was the discovery of active volcanoes on Io, a moon of Jupiter. Plumes of sulfur shoot 250 kilometers above Io's surface. In contrast, our moon has been a "dead" planetary body for three billion years, and no future volcanism is expected on it.

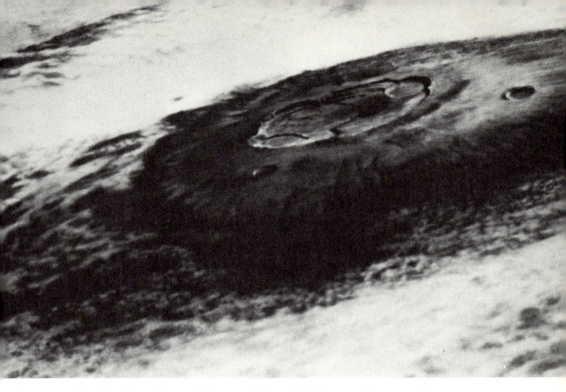

The Martian volcano, Olympus Mons, is the largest known volcano in the solar system.

Countless volcanoes then have erupted during the four and a half billion years of the solar system's lifetime. Today's volcanologists and geologists have classified them into types and identified the materials that are likely to erupt. They now understand why volcanoes form in the first place and can tell whether or not a particular volcano may erupt again in the near future and how dangerous that eruption is likely to be. They also have discovered how volcanism can actually benefit humankind.

29

◄ 2 ►

The Kinds of Volcanoes and Volcanism

Mild earthquakes are common on the volcanic island of Hawaii, but when scientists at Hawaii's Volcano Observatory recorded over 100 on February 24, 1955, they knew that the island was in for trouble. So many earthquakes in a region of active volcanoes always signals an imminent eruption. The place of unrest this time, scientists determined, was the east flank of monstrous Kilauea volcano, near the village of Kapoho and possibly right on the ranch of a man named Harold Warner.

Two days later the number of earthquakes reached an incredible 600 within twenty-four hours. The Warner family reported feeling quakes every few minutes and hearing booming noises and rumbles with each tremor. They also saw their ranch dogs acting strangely,

An eruption on Hawaii shoots lava as fountains 200 meters high.

burrowing and sniffing excitedly at the ground, possibly detecting volcanic gases seeping to the surface.

In two more days, a huge crack opened in the ground a few hundred feet from the Warner ranch, and fountains of lava shot from it to a height of twenty meters. Escaping gases whistled from the crack and hurled fragments of lava through the air as liquid globs. Cone-shaped hills grew as high as ten meters where the lava fell as bombs and cinders.

Unaccountably sparing the Warner ranch, the fountain eruptions instead threatened to overrun nearby Kapoho with molten rock rushing down Kilauea's

31

flanks like a river. Then more cracks opened—some one meter wide—and parts of the ground near Kapoho started to sink. One crack opened in the middle of the village, but not before the National Guard had evacuated the people. Soon there were seven new outbreaks of lava, one of which eventually destroyed the western section of Kapoho.

Outside the village, lava fountains reached a height of thirty meters, squirting as though shot from fire hoses. The fountains blazed red in the daylight and glowed like liquid gold at night. Scientists photographing the eruptions found the heat of the molten rock so strong that their cameras became too hot to hold. And the roar of the escaping gases made their ears ache.

Strangely, the dull plopping of still-liquid globs striking the ground was mingled with a crashing and rattling that sounded like dishes breaking. The reason was that the thousands of shreds of lava thrown out to the edges of the fountains chilled to volcanic glass, which then shattered against the ground.

The volcanic activity at Kapoho ceased about a week after it started. But Kilauea's rest was short. On March 13, new cracks broke open ten kilometers from Kapoho along the road between Pahoa and Kalapana. Guardsmen again moved in to evacuate residents, this time working around three steaming rivers of lava that poured down the volcano's flanks and into the sea.

Not until May 26 did Kilauea's east-flank activity completely stop. By that time, lava flows had destroyed all of one village, part of another, and buried 3,900 acres of rich farmland. This damage, although great, was much less than that caused by the Mount Saint Helens' eruption in May, 1980. And unlike the explosive Mount Saint Helens, Kilauea's 1955 eruption took no lives.

The difference in violence between these two volcanoes is due to the different ways in which they erupted. Altogether volcanologists recognize that there are five distinctive eruption styles. One is called Hawaiian, after the volcanoes of Hawaii, which mainly produce red-hot lava flows and fountains and have only mild explosive force.

A fiery, aa lava flow from Kilauea's 1955 eruption slowly moves across a field, burning vegetation.

The Strombolian eruption of Cerro Negro, Nicaragua, in 1968.

Slightly more explosive than a Hawaiian eruption is Strombolian volcanism. Typical Strombolian eruptions shoot glowing lapilli and bombs dozens of meters into the air, unlike the steady spray of lava fountains during Hawaiian eruptions. Gray clouds of ash rise from the volcano's summit several hundreds of meters high, and lava may pour from fractures near the base of the volcano. Strombolian eruptions are known for their "permanence," continually sputtering and showering the surrounding area with pyroclastic fragments for months or even years.

More violent than Strombolian volcanism is the Vulcanian type. Vulcanian eruptions commonly blast out hot blocks of old lava present as rock in the throat of a volcano, and then explode new magma into bombs, lapilli, and dark-colored ash clouds. The explosion clouds rise into giant cauliflower or pine-tree forms kilometers above the volcano. Afterward, winds move the clouds long distances, and the ash rains down on the countryside it passes over. Lava flows generally come at the end of a cycle of Vulcanian activity.

A particularly powerful and violent type of volcanism is known as Plinian. It is named after Pliny the Elder, who lost his life in the A.D. 79 eruption of Vesuvius. Like Vulcanian eruptions, Plinian volcanism also produces a tall, ash-rich cloud, but the energy of the eruption is equal to an atomic explosion and a large amount of pumice is erupted. Three meters of pumice, for example, buried Pompeii in A.D. 79. The Mount Saint Helens explosion of May 18, 1980, was also a pumice-rich Plinian eruption.

This 1944 eruption of Vesuvius is best described as
a Vulcanian type of eruption.

Peléan volcanism, the fifth kind, is highly violent and especially destructive. This type is named for the volcano Mont Pelée on the Caribbean island of Martinique. Mont Pelée was little known until it became restless early in April, 1902, shaking the island with earthquakes and shooting ash clouds from its summit. Suddenly ash started to pour down on the streets of Saint-Pierre, the city at the foot of the volcano, and the odor of sulfur permeated the air. By May, the ash had become so thick that it blocked roads and forced businesses to close. The poisonous gases and the ash were beginning to kill birds and smother small wildlife. On May 3, the local newspaper, *Les Colonies*, stated, "The rain of ashes never ceases. . . . The passing of carriages in the streets is no longer heard. . . . The wheels are muffled in the ash. . . . Puffs of wind sweep the ashes from the roofs and awnings, and blow them into rooms of which the windows have been left open. . . ."

As the morning of May 8 dawned great ash clouds were still rising from Mont Pelée. There was nothing unusual about the volcano to arouse suspicion in Saint-Pierre. But then, at 7:50 A.M., Mont Pelée erupted with four cannonlike shots, belching up a black cloud laced with lightning flashes. The steaming volcano issued yet another blast, this one sending a thick boiling cloud down the mountainside, an avalanche charged with ash and gases. Its temperature was about

The glowing avalanche from the 1902 eruption of Mont Pelée left Saint-Pierre, Martinique, a wasteland.

800 degrees Celsius. This "glowing avalanche" barreled over Saint-Pierre with hurricane speed and spread out over the sea. In a matter of seconds, the cloud claimed 30,000 lives and set the city afire. Those not killed instantly by the blast surely died in the fires. Only two men in Saint-Pierre survived: one was a pris-

oner in an underground dungeon, and the other was a shoemaker who miraculously escaped the flames that engulfed his home.

Of the seventeen ships in the harbor, fifteen capsized. The shock of the blast tore the British steamer *Roddam* free from its anchor, so its crew managed to escape to Saint Lucia. There twelve crewmen arrived dead and ten had to be hospitalized because of severe body burns. A survivor on the ship *Roraima* in the harbor reported that he saw "the rolling and leaping of red flames that belched from the mountain. . . . It was like the biggest

Damage caused by the glowing avalanche from Mount Lamington, Papua, New Guinea, 1951.

oil refinery in the world burning up on the mountain-top. . . . The mountain was blown to pieces. There was no warning. The side of the volcano was ripped out and there was hurled straight toward us a solid wall of flame."

Pelean eruptions then produce glowing avalanches. These highly heated clouds spill over the countryside up to 100 kilometers an hour, hugging the ground because they are loaded with ash and pumice fragments. The blanket of hot pyroclastic fragments laid down can still be warm a year after the eruption.

Whether or not a volcano erupts in the Hawaiian, Strombolian, Vulcanian, Plinian, or Peléan style depends largely on the chemical composition of the magma that comes to it from below. In particular, the amount of silicon, the main element in magmas aside from oxygen, influences what type of eruption will occur.

Geologists express the silicon content of magmas as an oxide called "silica." It is written SiO_2 in chemical symbols. The abundance of silica in magmas can be anywhere from 35 percent up to 75 percent (by weight). The less the silica content, the more fluid a magma will be. Some fluid magmas flow down slopes as lavas at speeds of several kilometers per hour. Most important, however, is that the more fluid a magma is, the more easily its gases can escape. Without high gas

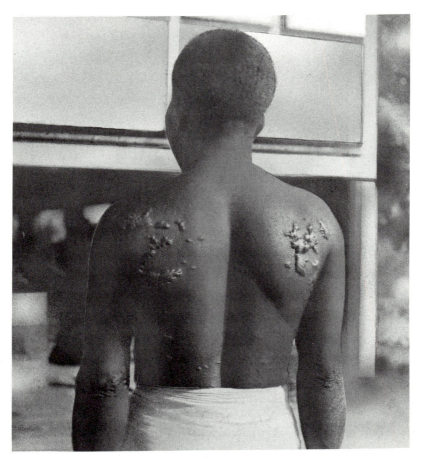

Burns inflicted on a victim of the glowing avalanche
from Mount Lamington, Papua, New Guinea, 1951.

pressures building up, volcanic eruptions are not explosive.

A common kind of magma that has low silica (less than about 55 percent) is called "basaltic," and the

The broad, gently sloped shield volcano Haleakala,
on Maui, Hawaiian Islands.

rock type that forms after it erupts and cools is known
as basalt. Because of the fluidity of basaltic magmas,
their eruptions are comparatively quiet and often of
the Hawaiian type. Large amounts of basaltic lava commonly develop broad and gently sloped volcanoes that
resemble shields. The foundations of all the Hawaiian
islands, for example, are shield volcanoes of basalt.

The shield volcanoes of ocean islands are massive
structures that extend kilometers down to the sea floor.
Mauna Loa, for instance, is much higher than the four
kilometers that rise above the Pacific Ocean. When
measured from the sea floor, it is ten kilometers high.
And, as demonstrated by Kilauea in 1955, shield erup-

tions do not necessarily occur at volcano summits but occur at flank fractures as well.

When an eruption of basaltic magma is largely pyroclastic, or Strombolian, a cinder cone forms. Escaping gases shoot up magma fragments, which then cool to cinders and accumulate around the vent in a cone shape. Cinder cones grow as isolated volcanoes and on top of shield volcanoes, such as at local eruptions on Kilauea. They are small compared to other volcanoes, usually less than 500 meters high and less than 1,500 meters in diameter at the base. But no matter what its size, a cinder cone always has a bowl-shaped crater at its summit.

Craters develop on cinder cones for two reasons. One is that the cinders thrown out fall back onto the walls around the vent and build the walls higher, while the force of the escaping gas helps clear the vent area of falling cinders. The second reason is that any magma removed leaves a hole, or void, inside the volcano into which the rock near the surface may then sink.

Magma having intermediate silica content (about 56 to 65 percent) is called "andesitic," and the rocks are known as andesite. When andesitic magma erupts, it makes tall, steep-sided, cone-shaped volcanoes. These large cones, however, are constructed of intermixed layers of lava flows and pyroclastic material, forming composite volcanoes. Eruption types at composite volcanoes are usually Strombolian, Vulcanian, Plinian or Peléan. Rarely are they Hawaiian.

Composite volcanoes are the most common type worldwide. In size, they can be several thousand meters high and up to thirty kilometers across at the base.

Two cinder cones in the San Francisco volcanic field near Flagstaff, Arizona. Crater 160 is in the foreground and SP crater and lava flow are in the background.

The eruption of the composite volcano Shishaldin,
Unimak Island, Alaska.

Mount Rainier in Washington, for instance, rises 3,600 meters above the surrounding landscape, and Mount Fuji in Japan is nearly 3,800 meters high. Other famous composite volcanoes are Vesuvius, Mount Etna, Stromboli, and Mount Saint Helens.

Like cinder cones, composite volcanoes grow by eruptions that come from a central pipe vent, and craters form at their summits. Whereas some craters develop from collapse, others are products of explosions, such as Mount Saint Helens' huge new crater. If magma ever plugs the vent of a composite volcano, later eruptions may sprout from a new vent that punctures the volcano's flanks. A smaller, parasite cone may then develop on the flanks, as Shastina did on the side of Mount Shasta in California.

Large volumes of magma that have erupted from some composite volcanoes have caused the collapse of an entire mountain, as happened to Mount Mazama, a majestic composite volcano active in Oregon 6,000 years ago. Slowly as pyroclastic and lava eruptions occurred the mountain grew to a height of 3,500 meters. Glaciers filled high valleys near its peak. Eventually, however, Mount Mazama became overactive with Plinian eruptions. The surrounding region was smothered by thick layers of ash and pumice, some hot enough to burn and carbonize trees over a fifty-kilometer distance. In time, the volume of magma blown out from the chamber below the volcano equaled about forty-five cubic kilometers, leaving a void large enough to fill with over 40,000 Empire State Buildings. Rock that overlay the magma no longer had support from below, and Mount Mazama collapsed. Left at the surface was a monstrous crater ten kilometers across. This super crater, or caldera, later filled with water and is now the popular tourist spot of Crater Lake.

Crater Lake, Oregon, formed 6,000 years ago from the collapse of Mount Mazama volcano.

Magmas of highest SiO_2 content (greater than 66 percent) are called "rhyolitic." They are the most viscous, meaning that they resist flow much more than water does. Viscous magma and lava behave like cold honey.

While in the Earth's crust, these viscous magmas barely allow gases to escape at all, causing rhyolitic magmas to erupt in one of two ways. If the gases that cannot escape build up extreme pressures, a sudden explosive eruption occurs. Plinian and Peléan eruptions are explosions of highly viscous magmas.

On the other hand, viscous rhyolitic magmas may only ooze from vents into huge piles of lava and form volcanic domes, the way cold toothpaste would behave

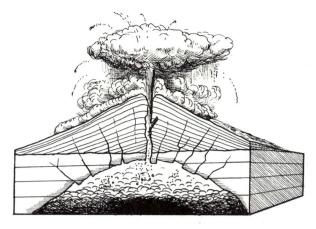

(a) Mount Mazama erupts, leaving a void in the magma chamber.

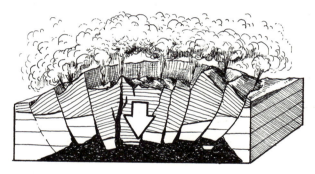

(b) Without support from below, the huge volcano collapses.

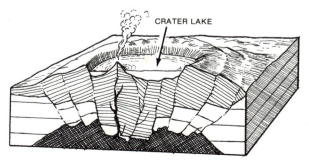

CRATER LAKE

(c) Water collects in the caldera to form a lake.

if squeezed from a vent. Rhyolitic lava rarely travels more than one or two kilometers from its vent.

Lassen Peak in California is an example of a great volcanic dome. Domes, however, sometimes form inside composite volcanoes when magma rises to plug a vent shortly after a Vulcanian, Plinian, or Peléan eruption has occurred. Frequently, however, these domes do not last long. Renewed pressures below eventually blast them out of the vent as ash and rock fragments. At Mount Saint Helens, for example, viscous lava plugged the vent after the great explosive eruption on May 18, but the plug was destroyed by an eruption on July 22, 1980.

Whether or not a magma erupts quietly or violently, or whether it forms a shield, dome, or a cone, water plays a big role in the volcanism. Not surface water, it is what geologists call "juvenile water." It comes from within the Earth and has never been on the surface before. Small amounts of juvenile water are present in all magmas and, in the form of vapor, make up most of the gas that erupts at volcanoes. In fact, over the long history of the Earth, water vapor escaping as volcanic gas has produced most of the atmosphere and oceans.

Juvenile water is important in volcanism because of what happens to water as it changes from liquid to vapor. During that change, its volume instantly in-

A volcanic dome is blasted out of Mount Lamington,
Papua, New Guinea.

creases 1,000 times. This drastic physical change of water in magmas occurs as magma rises, from where it forms at great depth, to a magma chamber below a volcano. Pressure on a rising magma gradually decreases, and the hot liquid water within it changes to vapor. If the vapor is confined and cannot expand in volume—which is likely to be the situation in a magma chamber—it will instead exert a tremendous pressure. Herein lies the main force behind volcanic eruptions.

◄3►

How Volcanoes Are Born

Nearly all reported volcanic eruptions have been at volcanoes that already existed. A volcano actually "blossoming" from level ground is rarely witnessed. In North America, for example, only two volcanoes have been born in historic time. Both sprouted up as cinder cones in western Mexico, where volcanoes already existed aplenty. Jorullo volcano formed in 1759, and Paricutín developed in 1943.

Paricutín's birth took place before the very eyes of Mexican farmer Dionisio Pulido as he worked his cornfields on the afternoon of February 20. After his farmland was shaken by earthquakes for two weeks, the volcanism struck as a half-meter deep fracture that ripped open the land. The ground immediately swelled to a level three meters higher than normal, and smoke and ash shot from portions of the fracture.

Within minutes, villagers three kilometers away saw

the plume rising high above what they knew to be only cornfields. Those who joined Pulido in the erupting cornfield were able to watch an area within the fracture gradually expand to two meters across while it spewed smoke and ash and spit cinders five meters high. As the vent grew even larger, however, the intense heat and the choking sulfur odor coming from it forced the observers away. Later that evening an entire community of farmers in the town of San Juan Parangaricutiro gazed disbelievingly as glowing bombs rocketed skyward from the vent and lightning flashed within the column of smoke. The cornfield had become an inferno.

Overnight the cinders piled up around the vent. By morning, Pulido discovered a ten-meter-high cinder cone on his land. By midday, Paricutín volcano reached fifty meters high and was issuing black, slag-like lava that oozed across the cornfield at five meters per hour. In its second day of life, Paricutín was displaying a Strombolian eruption.

At the end of the first week, Paricutín stood 140 meters tall and its explosive sounds could be heard 350 kilometers away. Every few seconds it ejected pyroclastic material including meter-sized bombs one kilometer high. By the following month, the ash and dust that Paricutín had been shooting from its crater powdered countryside up to 300 kilometers away. All this time lava flowed steadily from fractures near its

Paricutín sprouted up in a cornfield
in western Mexico in 1943.

base, burying the surrounding farmland deeper and
deeper.

At the end of its first year, Paricutín was 325 meters
above the cornfield where it had begun as a narrow
vent. Afterward, however, the growth rate slowed
greatly because the volcanism turned almost entirely
to eruptions of lava that spread out away from the cone.
When Paricutín finally quieted in 1952, it stood 410
meters high.

Paricutín's activity in Mexico enabled geologists to observe exactly how a volcano is born and how it gradually develops over time into a monumental structure. They watched as Paricutín put out an average of about one million tons of solid material a day, 27 percent of which was lava. And they saw how years of continuous lava activity eventually buried the nearby town of San Juan Parangaricutiro and how falling ash blanketed

Strombolian-type fireworks from Paricutín volcano.

the countryside a meter high for a distance of six kilometers.

But hidden from view at Paricutín, as at all other volcanoes, were the geologic processes below the surface that led to the eruption. These processes involve the formation and rising of the magma that broke out at the surface to build the volcano.

Below the surface, temperatures increase about one degree Celsius every thirty meters deeper into the Earth. At this rate, all rock should be molten at about thirty-five kilometers depth and deeper. Most subsurface rock, however, remains solid. The reason is that pressures increase downward, too, because of the growing thickness and weight of overlying rock. And because pressure works to keep rock solid, the temperatures needed to melt rock at depth and under pressure are much higher than would be needed at the surface.

Magma forms then whenever a local region of subsurface rock becomes too hot to stay solid even under high pressure. When these conditions for melting occur, the depth is usually between twenty-five to eighty kilometers beneath the surface, or in the lower crust and upper mantle. The crust is the Earth's outer layer, about fifty kilometers thick on the continents and about ten kilometers thick beneath the oceans. The mantle is the layer of rock below the crust that extends downward to the Earth's iron core 2,900 kilometers below.

Once magma forms, it is lighter (less dense) than surrounding rock and migrates upward. Often it accumulates in a chamber, or reservoir, near the surface, where gas pressures build up. As some of the magma erupts from the chamber and causes volcanism, new magma may rise from the zone of formation below to refill the chamber.

Not all magma reaches the surface, however. Some pockets of rising magma become trapped in the crust. There they cool and become part of it. On the other hand, the heat from rising magma may melt some crustal rock and form even more magma that eventually erupts at the surface.

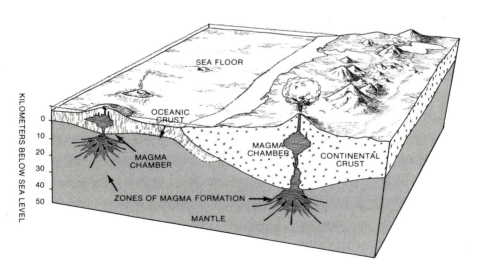

Zones of magma formation lie in the upper mantle and lower crust.

57

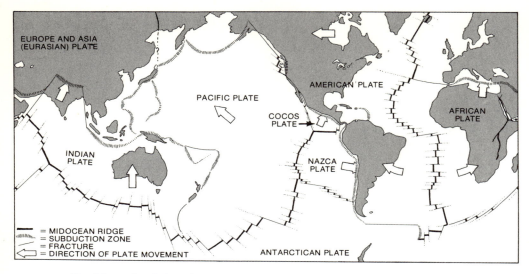

Earth's major lithospheric plates and their directions of movement.

Magma production and volcanism occur only in certain regions of the Earth. To explain why and where, geologists call upon the theory of plate tectonics.

This theory proposes that the Earth's outer one hundred kilometers of rock, consisting of crust and upper mantle and called the "lithosphere," are broken into several huge segments, or plates. These plates slowly move past, over, and under one another. The movement, which is only about two to five centimeters a year, causes the continents to drift across the face of the Earth and the sea floor to spread apart. It is also responsible for most volcanism, for in the regions where two plates collide or move apart, heat and pressure are often in the balance needed to allow melting of crustal or mantle rock and the formation of magma.

The western coast of Mexico is one area where two lithospheric plates meet head on. Their collision forces the Cocos plate, covered by oceanic crust, to slide beneath the North American plate, covered by continental crust. This movement has created a subduction zone, a geologic environment produced by one plate overriding another. As oceanic crust moves along this subduction zone and into the hot mantle beneath Mexico, it melts and forms magma. Paricutín is a product of that magma.

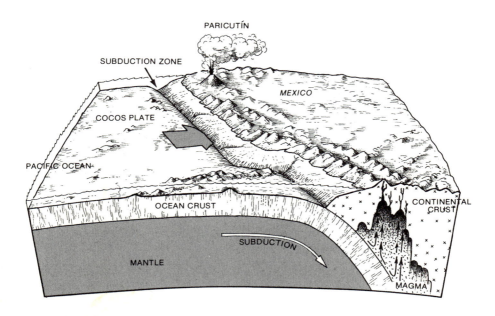

Formation of magma in the subduction zone beneath Mexico leads to volcanism at the surface.

Subduction zones almost surround the Pacific Ocean, marking where plates bearing oceanic crust pass beneath other lithospheric plates. The melting in these regions accounts for the hundreds of volcanoes around the Pacific, forming the so-called ring of fire.

Where sea floor thrusts beneath a continent, enough composite volcanoes and cinder cones may develop on the continental surface to form a mountain range. The Cascades Range in the Northwest, for example, is a product of the Gorda plate subducted beneath Washington and Oregon. The most recent evidence of magma formation there is Mount Saint Helens' activity.

The entire western coast of South America is another example. The Andes Mountains developed there because the Nazca plate has been moving beneath the South American plate for the past 100 million years.

Where a plate capped by oceanic crust passes beneath another plate having oceanic crust, a chain of volcanic islands forms on the ocean floor above the subduction zone. Geologists call these features "island arcs." Japan, the Aleutian Islands, and the West Indies are examples of island arcs.

Hundreds of the world's volcanoes are located where they are because of a subduction zone below that supplies magmas. In addition to those along the Pacific Ocean margin, there is another belt of subduction-

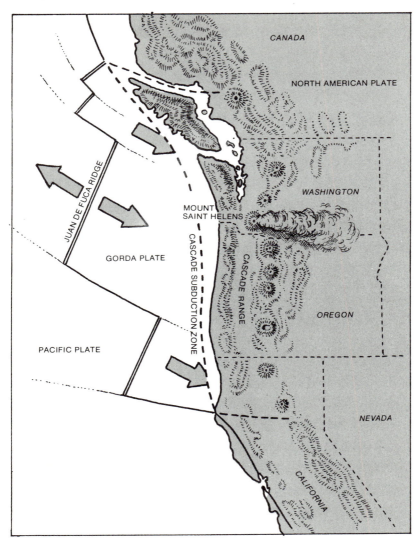

The Cascade Range, including Mount Saint Helens, developed because of a subduction zone beneath Oregon and Washington.

61

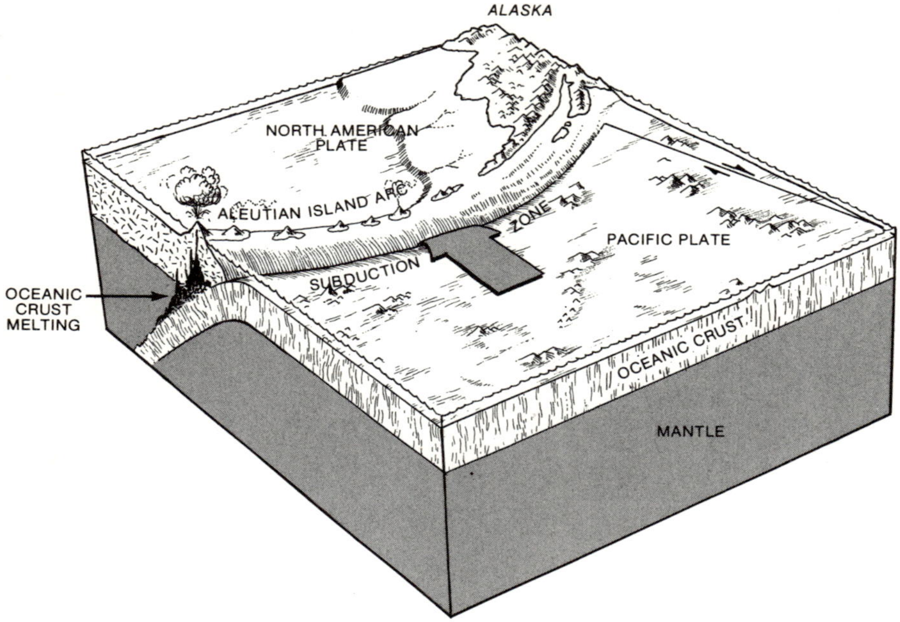
ALASKA
NORTH AMERICAN PLATE
ALEUTIAN ISLAND ARC
ZONE
PACIFIC PLATE
SUBDUCTION
OCEANIC CRUST MELTING
OCEANIC CRUST
MANTLE

The Aleutian peninsula, Alaska, is a volcanic island arc formed above a subduction zone.

related volcanoes in the Mediterranean Sea region of southern Europe and the Middle East.

Where two oceanic plates spread apart, magma from the mantle fills the gap between. Volcanism at these plate boundaries has created an almost continuous chain of volcanoes, 65,000 kilometers in length, along ocean floors of the globe. This "midocean ridge" system, as the entire volcanic mountain range is called, is up to 1,000 kilometers in breadth and stands up to

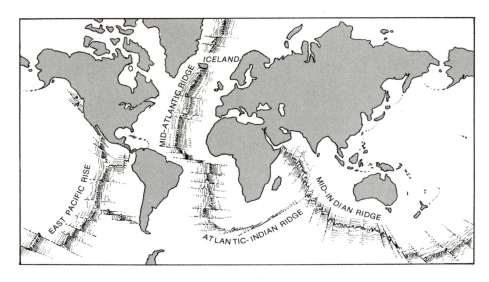

The midocean ridge system is a 65,000-kilometer volcanic mountain chain on the ocean floors.

4,000 meters above the sea floor. Portions are more massive and rugged than the Rocky Mountains.

Volcanism has been great enough along parts of the midocean ridge system to raise it above sea level. Iceland is an example. It is a huge volcanic island constructed from magma eruptions along the mid-Atlantic ridge. This ridge is the portion of the system that snakes along the Atlantic Ocean floor from north of Iceland to almost as far south as Antarctica. It formed because volcanism occurred—and still occurs—where the North and South American plates are spreading apart from the Eurasian and African plates.

Occasionally a new volcanic island will rise from a midocean ridge, as happened near Iceland in Novem-

Surtsey erupted on the mid-Atlantic ridge in 1963.

ber, 1963. The mid-Atlantic ridge erupted through 130 meters of water and constructed a 100-meter island overnight. The island, named Surtsey after an Icelandic mythological giant, actively spouted lava and pyroclastic material for nearly four years. Today it is about 2 square kilometers in size and over 150 meters high.

Surtsey's development was of interest to other scientists besides geologists. Biologists and botanists carefully monitored Surtsey to determine exactly what animal and plant life would be the first to arrive on the new island. Sea gulls made short stops on the island within two weeks, and by the summer of 1964 over a dozen bird species were spotted. Butterflies and flies were quick to find Surtsey too. Seeds washed ashore in 1964, and in June 1965 the first green rooted plant appeared in Surtsey soil. It was a plant named sea rocket, which grows on Iceland's sandy seashores.

The reason for volcanism at midocean ridges is unusually high heat in the mantle at these areas. Scientists believe that underlying the ridges are great concentrations of heat currents rising from deep in the mantle. These "convection cells" of heat, as they are called, not only cause volcanism, they may be the forces driving the lithospheric plates.

Volcanism also occurs where continents split. The East African rift, for example, marks where Africa began to break apart more than ten million years ago. Among the numerous volcanoes in this rift valley are the famous Kilimanjaro and Mount Kenya.

Not all active volcanoes are found along plate boundaries. A small percentage occur above hot spots that are located randomly in the mantle, away from plate margins. One hot spot lies beneath the center of the Pacific plate, directly under the island of Hawaii. It is the reason for the volcanoes Kilauea and Mauna Loa, that make up much of the island. This single hot

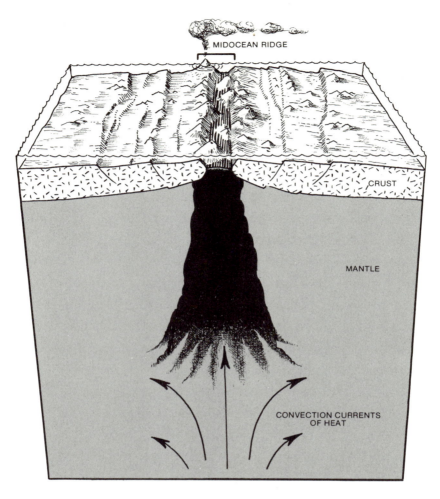

MIDOCEAN RIDGE

CRUST

MANTLE

CONVECTION CURRENTS
OF HEAT

Rising currents of heat may be the reason
for the volcanic midocean-ridge system.

spot also created the other principal Hawaiian islands
lying northwest of Hawaii: Maui, Molokai, Oahu, and
Kauai.

The reason that the Hawaiian Islands are lined up

66

in a row, even though they all came from the same magma source, is because the Pacific plate has been gradually moving in a northwesterly direction over that hot spot. Thus, after each volcanic island formed, the moving plate carried it away from its magma source in the mantle, the way wind passing over a chimney carries off puffs of smoke.

The scientific proof lies in the ages of the islands. Hawaii is less than one million years old, while Kauai, the island farthest from Hawaii, is about five million years old. The islands between have ages of one to three million years.

With time, islands drifting away from their magma sources erode. When worn low enough to be drowned

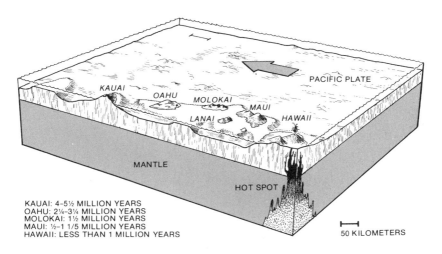

PACIFIC PLATE

KAUAI
OAHU
MOLOKAI
MAUI
LANAI
HAWAII

MANTLE

HOT SPOT

KAUAI: 4–5½ MILLION YEARS
OAHU: 2¼–3¼ MILLION YEARS
MOLOKAI: 1½ MILLION YEARS
MAUI: ½–1 1/5 MILLION YEARS
HAWAII: LESS THAN 1 MILLION YEARS

50 KILOMETERS

The hot spot beneath Hawaii created all the Hawaiian islands.

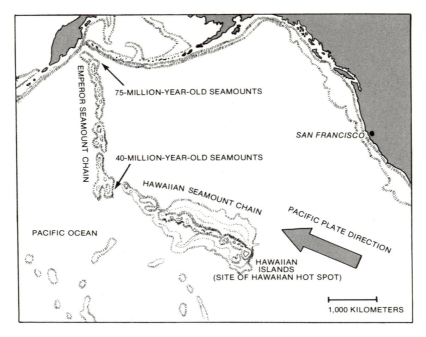

The Hawaiian and Emperor seamount chains represent volcanoes
formed on the sea floor over the past seventy-five million years.
Each volcano formed over the Hawaiian hot spot
and was slowly transported away by movement of the Pacific plate.

by the ocean, they become seamounts. The ages of the
seamounts that extend in a chain for 3,500 kilometers
northwest of the Hawaiian Islands strengthen the evidence for the theory that the Pacific plate is drifting
over a hot spot that produces volcanic islands. The
seamounts in the chain become progressively older in
a northwest direction.

Moreover, at about 3,500 kilometers from Hawaii,

68

the seamount chain changes direction and runs to the north. The seamounts near the elbow in the chain are about forty million years old. Geologists have concluded, therefore, that the Pacific plate moved in a northerly direction while passing over the Hawaiian hot spot until forty million years ago. The chain of volcanic islands that formed between forty and seventy-five million years ago have long eroded and are now the Emperor Seamounts.

◂4▸

Volcanoes and Humankind

During the 1955 Kilauea eruption, pumice, ash, and cinders from one of the main vents rained down for several weeks on a nearby patch of banana trees. In a short time, the broad leaves turned to limp shreds and the trees looked close to dead. The heat and the ash had certainly suffocated them, and the agricultural loss to the volcano seemed sure to be great.

But only one month after the eruption had stopped, the banana patch was amazingly healthy. Rather than destroy the plants, the pyroclastic material had helped their growth. Not only had it held rainwater for the trees to use, it acted as fertilizer.

Soil scientists recognize that all over the world layers of small pyroclastic particles produce fertile agricultural land. The reason is because ash is glassy material that readily breaks down and releases nutrients that plants need, such as potassium and phosphor-

Volcanic ash blankets the countryside in Costa Rica.

ous. Initially, crops may be damaged or even destroyed when lightly covered by volcanic ash. In Washington State, for instance, Mount Saint Helens' dust claimed many spring gardens. But usually the vegetation in ash-covered ground becomes more luxuriant in the following growing season. Lava flows, however, are a different story. Volcanic rock needs many years of weathering before its surface breaks down to soil that yields lush vegetation.

For both farm and wild animals, the immediate

effects of falling pyroclastic material can be disastrous. Grazing animals can starve if their food sources are deeply buried. Eating vegetation covered with ash can harm their digestive tracts. Animals can also grind their teeth away by eating vegetation mixed with ash, for the glassy particles are abrasive. In fact, pumice is abrasive enough for commercial purposes. The Proctor and Gamble Company, for example, uses pumice in their Lava Soap as a scouring agent.

Ash accumulations are harmful to buildings when they weigh heavily on rooftops. Ash can also clog and abrade aircraft and automobile engines. It contributes to the contamination of water supplies by plugging drains.

Soon after Mount Saint Helens erupted, residents of the Northwest became deeply concerned about health hazards posed by breathing volcanic dust. People wearing protective dust-particle masks while cleaning up the ash were familiar sights in towns like Yakima, Castle Rock, and Longview, Washington. Scientific tests, however, showed that the dust particles were small enough for the body to absorb eventually and that they presented no immediate danger to the respiratory system. But no one knows the long-term effects of breathing in a sudden dose of volcanic ash. The biggest concern is for silicosis, a lung disease caused by continued inhalation of silica (SiO_2) dust.

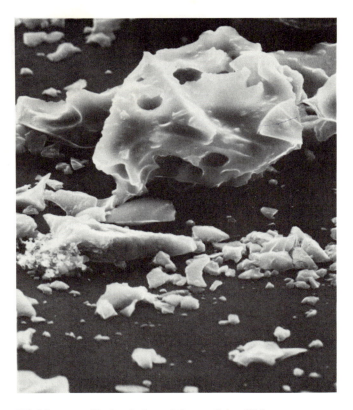

Highly magnified ash from Mount Saint Helens.
The size of the large jagged fragment is one-twentieth of a millimeter.

Volcanic eruptions can also affect the environment by causing changes in climate. In 1816, for instance, so much ash erupted from the Indonesian volcano Tambora that it brought a "year without a summer." The ash filled the sky and greatly reduced the amount of sunlight and heat reaching the Earth's surface.

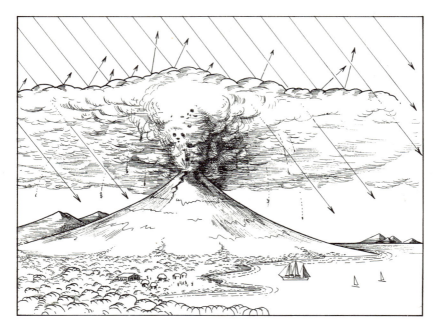

A large blast of volcanic ash into the atmosphere
can block out enough sunlight to cool the climate.

Three days of complete darkness fell over neighboring
areas such as Madura, an island 500 kilometers away.

The Tambora ash in the atmosphere was responsible
for cyclonic activity across Newfoundland, Ireland,
and England, resulting in almost steady rain from May
to October of 1816. In London, monthly temperatures
were two to three degrees Celsius cooler than normal.
Snow fell in New England between June 6 and 11, and

frosts occurred throughout the summer months. Crops did not ripen in parts of Europe and North America, and severe food shortages developed.

Even the Mount Saint Helens eruption, which pro-

A satellite view of Mount Saint Helens' volcanic ash
filling the atmosphere over Washington
six and one-half hours after the eruption on May 18, 1980.

duced only one eightieth of the ash that Tambora did, affected the world climate. However, the temporary change in climate was less than one tenth of a degree Celsius—too small to be noticeable.

Because a thick volcanic ash layer can reduce the amount of heat reaching the Earth from the sun, some scientists have proposed that periods of much volcanism in the past may have caused the ice ages. They suggest that with sunlight partially blocked out, the world climate could have cooled enough to enable huge ice sheets and mountain glaciers to grow. The more widely held belief, however, is that shifts in the Earth's orbit around the sun and in the Earth's axial tilt were responsible for cooling the climate and causing ice ages.

Lava flows offer their share of damage and danger too. Like rivers, lava seeks the lowest course for travel. Valleys, therefore, are the first areas that lava streams invade.

One of the earliest attempts to stop a lava flow was in Sicily in 1669. Lava from Mount Etna threatened to spill downhill into the town of Catania sixteen kilometers away. To save the city, several dozen residents covered themselves with wet cowhides for protection from the heat and walked up the volcano's slope to the lava flow. At a place where the lava's sidewall had already cooled and hardened, they dug an opening through the hot rock wall with iron bars. The lava then escaped from the side and began to flow in a new direction.

Unfortunately, the lava headed toward the town of Paterno. This action angered the citizens there, and about 500 men marched up the volcano to chase the Catania men away from the opening. Left unattended, the hole in the wall clogged and the lava once again descended toward Catania and destroyed a large section of the city.

Nearly 300 years later the United States Air Corps

Lava moves down a slope from Paricutín volcano in Mexico.

A blocky lava flow from Paricutín volcano
entered the town of San Juan Parangaricutiro.

used twentieth-century technology to change the course
of a Hawaiian lava flow. In 1935, they dropped twenty
600-pound bombs on a lava flow advancing 250 meters
per hour toward Hilo, the main city on the island of
Hawaii. The bombing broke open the sidewall of the
flow, and lava began to gush in another direction. The
next day lava approached Hilo at only 15 meters per
hour, and it completely stopped a half day later.

Barriers can stop lava flows effectively. In 1960, for
example, a bulldozer crew spent nine days piling up

rubble to make a 4-kilometer wall that later blocked a flow coming from a Kilauea vent. The lava actually poured over the wall, but the barrier did contain some of the flow and so helped reduce damage that might otherwise have occurred.

At some volcanoes, avalanches and mudflows present as much danger as lava flows and ash falls. For example, snows that suddenly melt from volcanic heat can lubricate steep slopes of snow or rock and send them roaring down the flanks and through nearby valleys. Rainfall after an eruption can drench thick ash layers, turning them into rivers of mud, as happened when the Vesuvius eruption covered Pompeii. The city of Herculaneum was not in the direct path of the destructive ashfall but was buried about two days following the eruption when mudflows up to twenty meters thick poured off the slopes of Vesuvius.

In a modern example, walls of ash, mud, and rocks from Mount Saint Helens raced fifty kilometers an hour down the Toutle River on the day of the big blast. These mudflows killed motorists, snapped highway bridges, and swept away homes and heavy logging equipment.

Although the heat of active volcanoes and their magmas is destructive, scientists recognize that there may someday be a way to harness some of it for the useful purpose of providing energy. The idea is to drill

This mudflow filled a river valley in Washington
after the eruption of Mount Saint Helens in May, 1980.

directly into a magma chamber, such as those beneath some volcanoes in Hawaii and Alaska, and insert a device to extract heat directly. But this heat-extraction technology is far from becoming a reality. One big problem lies in preparing a material that can survive the high temperatures—more than 650 degrees Celsius —and the corrosive actions of magmas for long periods.

On the other hand, present-day technology is capable of using the heat that remains underground in former volcanic regions. One operating example is at The Geysers in northern California, where a geothermal power plant was established in the 1920's. The site was discovered in 1847 when William Elliot was hunting grizzly bear in the Mayacamas Mountains 120 kilometers north of San Francisco. By chance, he came across a canyon with bubbling hot springs and hissing fumaroles, or small vents, that shot steam into the air. Elliot believed he had stumbled onto the "gates of hell."

California businessmen later put the natural hot water at The Geysers to use as a health spa. But by the early twentieth century, other businessmen made new plans for the steaming fumaroles. They recognized that the power of this steam shooting up from a well could turn turbines to generate electricity.

The first drilling in 1921 produced a sixty-five-meter well that had steam pressure of nearly five kilograms per square centimeter. That power was used to drill a

A 110,000-kilowatt geothermal power plant at
The Geysers, California.

second, deeper well that had about the same steam pressure. By 1925, eight steam wells had been drilled, each one capable of delivering about 1,000 kilowatts of electricity. Today the Pacific Gas and Electric Company obtains over 1,000 megawatts of electricity, or more than half of San Francisco's needs, from about 100 wells in operation at The Geysers.

Geologists have determined that the heat producing the steam at The Geysers comes from a giant magma body buried about five to eight kilometers below the surface. It is the same magma that erupted more than a million years ago to emplace the volcanic rock formations in the region. The steam forms because groundwater seeping downward becomes heated under pressure to temperatures far above the normal boiling temperature of water (100 degrees Celsius). Heated and lighter (less dense), the water migrates to the surface along fractures in the Earth's crust. Water that retains its high temperature, above the boiling point, while rising will blast out of the ground as steam.

Geothermal areas such as The Geysers, however, are rare. In all likelihood, The Geysers will be the only natural steam area ever to produce electricity in the United States. Yellowstone National Park has hot springs, fumaroles, and geysers, but they will never be used for producing electricity because Yellowstone is a national park. Elsewhere sizable geothermal power

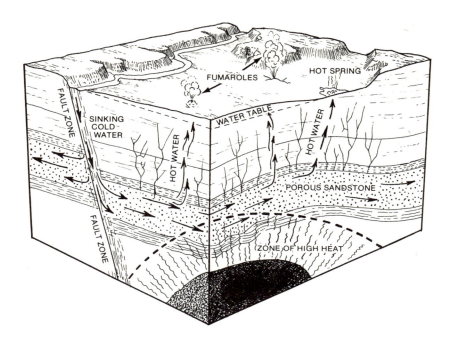

Water heated in the crust by magma bodies rises to form
steam vents (fumaroles) and hot springs at the surface.

plants are operating in New Zealand, Italy, and Iceland.

On the other hand, almost any area where volcanism occurred during the last few million years can become a geothermal source of energy. Hot rock or a magma body that is cooling lies below these areas at relatively shallow depths. What is needed for energy production, however, is groundwater that is heated by the buried heat source and that then rises to the surface. Or if groundwater does not naturally circulate back up to the surface, scientists can try to inject water and force it to circulate to and from hot rock below the surface. Geologists at Los Alamos Scientific Laboratory in New Mexico undertook such a project in the early 1970's.

The area selected for this hot dry rock geothermal well was practically at the back door of the lab in the one-million-year-old Valles volcanic field. Calculations and geologic studies had showed that a cooling magma body lay below the surface and that the temperature of water at the depth of three kilometers would be high above the normal boiling point. The task then was to send water down, heat it, and bring it back.

The scientists drilled two 3,300-meter-deep holes about 75 meters apart. Then, using an oil-field technique called "hydraulic fracturing," they shattered the rock at the bottom of the drill holes so that small channelways would connect the two wells. In this way, water pumped down one hole would move through the fractures to the other well while being heated by the hot rock nearly three kilometers below. Once heated, the water would rise up the second hole to the surface.

The hot dry project was successful by 1980. Water having a temperature of about 135 degrees Celsius rises to the surface at a rate of 375 liters per minute. At the surface, it passes through a heat exchanger that

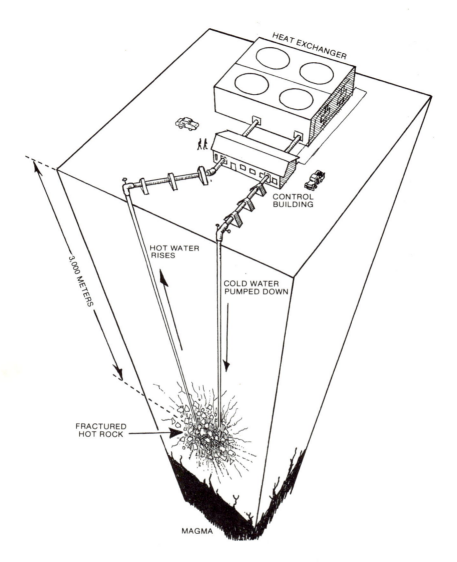

Near Los Alamos, New Mexico, water is forced downward to become heated by a deep magma. Upon rising, it is recovered and used for its heat energy.

86

generates enough electricity to light up several buildings.

While some scientists are working to use more volcanic regions for geothermal energy, others are watching volcanoes for signs of activity and possible eruption. Earthquake activity is probably the clearest signal of a coming eruption, for small quakes almost always precede volcanism. However, in 1975, Mount Baker volcano in Washington State exhibited the first signs of renewed activity as increased heat at the summit. Residents and hikers in the region noticed an increase in the number of fumaroles and the formation of a crater lake.

Mount Baker never did explode, but geologists have been keeping careful watch over it ever since. Their work includes using seismographs, for detecting even the weakest earthquakes, and tiltmeters. The tiltmeter measures bulging or swelling in the flanks of a volcano caused by magma rising within. It can measure ground movements of less than a millimeter.

Another instrument used for helping predict volcanic eruptions, particularly on Hawaii, is the laser geodimeter. It uses a laser beam to detect bulging. Magnetometers and gravity meters are also helpful because changes in the magnetic and gravity measurements around a volcano can indicate whether a magma body is rising into it.

Scientists plan to keep watch on Mount Saint Helens with instruments that can detect bulging due to magma pressure building below.

At some volcanoes, scientists have found that the compositions of gases escaping from fumaroles can help predict eruptions. At two fumaroles on Kilauea, for example, the amount of helium compared to the amount of carbon dioxide in the gases seeping from the fumaroles notably decreased several weeks before some eruptions in the 1970's.

The Earth can flare up anywhere along its belts of active volcanoes. No instruments or observations can determine exactly when an eruption will happen. But sudden earthquake activity and changes in temperatures, ground tilt, and gas compositions can alert scientists to a potential eruption. They can then warn the public of the possible hazards. With early notice, people can do much to spare themselves the danger and disaster that come when the Earth is afire.

Glossary

aa: a lava flow having an angular, jagged surface.

andesite: a volcanic rock type having 56 to 65 percent silica (SiO_2) content, mainly associated with composite volcanoes.

ash: particles of erupted magma less than two millimeters in size.

basalt: a volcanic rock type having less than 55 percent silica (SiO_2) content, commonly associated with "quiet" eruptions at shield volcanoes.

blocks: angular pyroclastic material greater than sixty-four millimeters in size, erupted as solid rock.

bombs: pyroclastic material, greater than sixty-four millimeters in size, erupted in a liquid or plasticlike form and acquiring spherical or twisted shapes during flight or flattened shapes upon hitting the ground.

caldera: a large (several kilometers in size) circular depression in a volcanic region.

cinder cone: a cone-shaped hill built largely of loose pyroclastic material surrounding a volcanic vent.

cinders: loose pyroclastic fragments forming a volcanic gravel.

composite volcano: a large volcanic cone built of alternating layers of lava and pyroclastic material.

crater: a bowl-shaped feature at the summit of a volcano.

crust: the outermost layer of the Earth's rock, about ten kilometers thick beneath the oceans and about fifty kilometers thick beneath the continents.

dome: a large, upside-down-bowl-shaped pile of lava or volcanic rock.

earthquake: motion or shaking of the ground set off by a sudden, great disturbance in the crust or upper mantle.

fumarole: a small vent in the ground that issues volcanic gases and heated groundwater but no lava.

geothermal: pertaining to the heat of the Earth's interior.

hot spot: an isolated hot place in the mantle that continually produces magma over millions of years of time.

island arc: a chain of volcanic islands formed over a subduction zone.

lapilli: loose pyroclastic material two millimeters to sixty-four millimeters in size.

laser geodimeter: an instrument that measures ground tilt by using a laser beam.

lava: magma, or molten rock, that has reached the surface.

lithosphere: the Earth's outer 100 kilometers of rock, which includes both the crust and the upper mantle.

magma: molten rock below the Earth's surface.

magma chamber: a huge reservoir below the Earth's surface, usually within a few kilometers below a volcano, where magma resides before erupting to the surface.

mantle: the main zone of the Earth's interior, extending from beneath the crust to a depth of 2,900 kilometers.

midocean ridge: an undersea mountain range formed by volcanism where two lithospheric plates spread apart.

mudflows: a large "soupy" movement of water and mud, much of which can be made of volcanic material.

pahoehoe: a lava flow having a rippled, ropy surface.

pillow lava: lava that cools underwater and acquires a surface resembling a pile of pillows or sandbags.

plate tectonics: the theory that the Earth's lithosphere is broken into plates that move, and the relationship of the moving plates to volcanism, earthquakes, and mountain building.

pumice: rock or fragments of volcanic glass filled with holes from which gases have escaped, giving it a spongy, frothy appearance.

pyroclastic: pertaining to fragments of volcanic material explosively erupted during volcanism.

rhyolite: a volcanic rock type having high silica (SiO_2) content, erupted either as a viscous dome or cloud of pyroclastic material.

seamount: an isolated mountain on the sea floor that is probably a submerged shield volcano.

shield volcano: a large, broad volcano with gentle slopes, composed mainly of basalt.

silica: the combination of one atom of the element silicon and two atoms of the element oxygen to form silicon dioxide, SiO_2, the main chemical component of magmas.

subduction zone: the zone in the lithosphere where one lithospheric plate sinks beneath another.

tiltmeter: an instrument that measures tilting or bulging in the Earth's crust.

tuff: a rock made of pyroclastic material, namely ash and pumice.

vent: an opening or pipelike channelway in the Earth's crust through which magma or gases erupt.

volcano: a cone-shaped hill or mountain built around a vent that connects with a reservoir of magma below.

Index

Vulcan, 17
Vulcanian eruption. *See*
   eruptions
Vulcano, 17

Warner, Harold, 30
water, 49, 51, 83

Yellowstone National Park, 83